CONFIDENT BUSINESS WRITING

A 7-Step Plan to Help You Overcome Your Business Writing Challenges

By Peter Clarke

Published by:
PPG Proofreading Ltd
Knowle
Fareham
Hants

First published in 2016
Copyright © Peter Clarke 2016

ISBN: 9781849148870

Note: The material contained in the book is set out in good faith for general guidance and no liability can be accepted for loss or expense incurred as a result of relying in particular circumstances on statements made in this book.

Front Cover: Purplelily Design, Southampton, Hants, www.purplelilydesign.co.uk.

About the Author

Peter Clarke lives in Hampshire, UK and has helped numerous businesses to ensure that everything they WRITE is RIGHT and free from errors.

Peter has run his own business for more than 10 years and is ideally placed to understand the challenges faced by small business owners on a daily basis.

He is a trained proofreader and copy editor and focusses on helping businesses to publish accurate and error-free copy regardless of whether it is paper or screen-based.

He is also a bid writer, helping organisations to develop project ideas and then assisting them to apply for funding from such sources as the European Social Fund. He has significant experience in working with project partners to ensure that delivery and expenditure is compliant with EU funding regulations and audit requirements.

He is also a travel writer and photographer and has published his own unique series of pocket sized travel guides under the banner of Peter's Pocket Guides alongside 2 e-books published as a result of his travels.

Contents

Introduction

Why you need this book

Do you break out into a cold sweat when faced with having to write something in your business?

Are you always stretched by a lack of time in your business and, as a result, the quality of your business writing suffers?

Do you wake up in the middle of the night worried about your business and whether something you have written will achieve the desired outcomes?

If so, rest assured, you're not alone.

There are many small business owners who, for one reason or another, are challenged when it comes to writing something in their businesses.

Everything you write in your business whether it's on a screen or on paper is either directly promoting or reflecting back on the quality of your business. It will also impact on how your prospective customers view you and your business.

The importance of getting your business writing accurate and error-free is paramount if you are going to achieve your goals.

In this book you will discover how to overcome your challenges through using a simple 7-step plan that will help your business to grow by attracting new customers with error-free writing and content.

This book is for you if:

-   You are a small business owner

-   Your business writing is a challenge for whatever reason

-   You could have a simple process plan to follow when you are writing something in your business that will help to alleviate your worries.

The purpose of this book

The purpose of this book is to highlight not only the continued importance of business writing in an era of rapidly changing technologies but also to recognise the challenges facing small business owners and their effect on business writing.

It is vital not to lose the traditional infrastructure that is found in correct business writing even though we are having to change and adapt it to meet the demands of technological advances, especially in the world of social media.

It remains vital that we, at the very least, get our spelling and grammar right if we are going to develop our businesses. So, if people are challenged with writing, it is perfectly OK and they should not be stigmatised in any way.

Business owners and their employees all need to be able to identify their strengths and weaknesses when it comes to not just business writing, but writing in general.

Writing for many is like riding a bike. Once you've got the hang of it there's no stopping you. You don't think twice when you pick up a pen or pencil; you just start putting your words down on paper.

For many, however, it's not like that. For many, writing is a real challenge and if it can be avoided, people will choose to do something else. In the modern era of computer technology, we don't have to pick up that dreaded pen or pencil. We can tap away at a keyboard and let the computer do the rest.

It's not that easy though. There's that old saying about computers: 'You only get out what you put in - put rubbish in and you'll get rubbish out'. Even Auto-Correct functions and spellcheckers are not fool-proof and should never be relied upon.

So, the challenge is still there even though the use of pen and paper is declining. Personally, when I write, I write using a pencil and paper in longhand. That's just me, though. It's what I'm comfortable with; it's what I've always done. In the days before computers, there was no alternative. Yes, I can remember those days!

I appreciate that today's generations are being brought up to use a keyboard or voice recognition software and maybe that's a contributory factor to why many people are challenged by spelling, grammar and the like. They are reliant on the technology to do it all for them.

As a trained copy editor and proofreader working with a variety of businesses, I see a wide range of abilities when it comes to business writing.

What do I mean by 'business writing'? Well, anything that is written in the day to day running of a business. It may be written on paper or on a screen. Whatever it is, that writing will either be directly promoting the business or it will be reflecting back on the quality of the business. Hence, in my opinion, it must be right otherwise the business will suffer because it will struggle to attract new customers.

Business writing can include any of the following:

Letters	Training	Questionnaires
Emails	handouts	Cover letters
Memos	Direct mail	Personal
Blogs	Press releases	statements
Articles	Media kits	Brochures
Reports	Sales pitches	Handbooks
Proposals	Funding	Social media
White papers	applications	content
E-books	Tender	Meeting minutes
Books	responses	Announcements
Newsletters	Business plans	Apologies
Website	CVs	
content		

And many more.........................

Business writing is also about how documents are structured and laid out. It's all well and good to write a 5,000 word report but if it consists of one long screed of text with little or no punctuation, paragraphs, sections with sub-headings etc., the reader will soon be turned off and the purpose and impact of the report will be lost.

Whilst things like spelling and grammar are generally taught in our schools, other aspects of business writing are not unless it is something learned at University. Not everyone, however, is fortunate enough to go to University.

My experience

I went straight into the world of work when I left school back in the mid-Seventies as going to University was an option I chose to forego at the time. In hindsight, now I see what my children have gained from a University education, I have some regrets about that decision. Be that as it may, at the time I chose to enter the world of banking at the bottom of the ladder as a statement clerk and over the years worked my way towards the top through hard work and learning which stood me in excellent stead for when I started my own business 15 or so years ago.

I will be forever grateful for the basic grounding that I learned especially when it came to writing in a business context. I am of the opinion today that many youngsters entering the workplace for the first time are not given the same grounding that I had all those years ago. OK, the culture in the workplace is different today and the requirements for traditional forms of business writing are different, but nevertheless, it's vital that basic spelling and grammar are right.

Working in an era before computers and email, I was brought up to write business letters, not only to customers but also to other departments of the Bank. I soon learned that customer letters were more informative in their content whereas departmental letters were more instructional, asking for things to be done on behalf of a customer. So, even at that young age, I was learning not only about the words to use but also about how the letter should be structured.

Nowadays, a traditional business letter is not commonly used, it having been largely superseded by email. Yes, emails can be a little less formal, nevertheless, I believe that a degree of formality is still required if that is your business's chosen form of communication and especially if it is the initial communication with a prospective customer.

Times are a-changing, however. The culture within our workplaces is changing as new technology comes in and advances so quickly. It's often difficult to keep up but unless you do keep up it's very easy to be left behind.

That's why we see a lot of young people coming into the workplace who are 'tech-savvy' and are given responsibilities which some may say are too advanced for their age. As a result, the quality of any written communications may not be as high as the management might expect, which can cause difficulties.

With the dawning of the age of social media and the way in which the English language is used on the plethora of available platforms, the style of business writing is changing, yet again. So, by and large, gone are the traditional business letters which have been replaced by the likes of emails, blogposts and website content. Social media content, such as Twitter, Facebook, Google+ and LinkedIn all command their own styles in which language is used. Spelling and grammar are suffering as a result and there is a tendency towards favouring speed and immediacy of delivery and response as against getting the words right.

What will you learn?

Many people have many different issues which makes writing difficult. People who are dyslexic; people for whom English is not their first language; people who have literacy and numeracy difficulties are all challenged when it comes to writing. It is important, therefore, that in a business environment these difficulties are recognised and that help is available in many ways to ensure that the individual and the business can be developed in the most advantageous way.

I'll look at some of the challenges that small business owners have to deal with and how these challenges can affect their business writing. I'll also look at the consequences of not dealing with these challenges and then offer some potential solutions to help overcome the challenges so that both individuals and businesses are able to develop.

I'll introduce you to the Business Writing Process Plan (BWPP) which is a 7-step process designed to help you consciously think about what you are writing and why and to make sure that, when it comes to publishing your writing, the quality of the end product is high.

This book will also help you to understand that you can't be an expert in everything especially when it comes to a topic as specific as business writing. You may have an area of expertise that is different to many other people and therefore that should be your area of focus to boost self-esteem and confidence. At the same time, there are people out there who know more about the things that you might be struggling with and that it's perfectly OK to admit to your limitations and to use their expertise to help you to achieve your goals.

There are experts out there who can help with content/copy writing. There are experts out there who can help you to edit what you write and there are experts out there who can check and proofread what you have written to make sure that it is right BEFORE you have it published or you send it off to your customer. After all, there is nothing more embarrassing than when your customer notices a mistake in what you have written.

Challenges facing small business owners

Setting up your own business and being your own boss, is probably a dream come true for many people.

It's not until the business has been running for a while when the inevitable thoughts start creeping into your mind that it's not as easy as you had originally anticipated.

Being self-employed and the owner of your own business means that you are responsible for everything, whether you know what you are doing, or not. Often, everything else gets in the way of you being able to actually do what you set up the business for in the first place.

Business writing is just one element of running a business and a very important one, so whatever challenge is thrown up will inevitably impact on the quality of the writing.

So, what sorts of challenges do small business owners face and how do these challenges impact on business writing?

Multi-hat wearing

A business owner is responsible for every aspect of the business so has to wear a variety of different hats every day, often at the same time. Whilst you are trying to focus on making the product or delivering the service, there's everything else that goes with running a business competing for your time. Things like marketing, finance, sales, HR and legal issues and many more are all essential aspects of a business and won't go away.

Many of these activities are a complete mystery to some business owners and therefore they need to seek help from people who know more about them than they do. Some business owners muddle through as best they can and that's when other problems can arise which will also affect their writing and how this reflects back on the quality of the business.

Reputation

People learn about your business often by what is written about it. Not all new business comes by way of referral. You will be spending a lot of time building up your reputation, both personal and for your business. Why waste all that time and effort and damage your reputation by forgoing the quality of what you write about your business? People pick up on mistakes and remember them, as well as telling their associates by posting a negative online review, maybe, so by taking a little extra care over what you write is time well spent.

Trying to be good at everything

What's wrong with being a 'jack of all trades and master of none'? I think that's perfectly OK as long as you are the master of the one thing you set up your business for in the first place. As there are so many variables when it comes to running a business it's impossible to be good at everything.

Business writing may not be one of your strong points for a variety of reasons. Rest assured, you're not alone. That's why there are people out there who are good at business writing – copy and content writers. Don't be afraid to ask them for help.

Ability to adapt to technological advances

Business writing has had to evolve with technological advances. With the advent of the Internet and emails and now social media, the way in which we express ourselves through our writing has changed. What you write on social media should be differentiated from what you write via emails and other forms of business communication.

Traditional business letters, whilst they are still used, have declined in number quite dramatically with the growth of email and other electronic communication. Being able to keep up with the speed of technological change is one thing but being able to adapt the style of our writing to the plethora of electronic media available to us is an altogether different thing.

That's why we are seeing a burgeoning growth of digital marketing businesses over recent years. Being tech-savvy business owners, there is an ever increasing market for providing services to those who are struggling to keep pace with the changes.

Dyslexia

Dyslexia is a specific learning difficulty that primarily affects the ability to learn to read and spell. It affects different people in different ways and some 10% of the UK population are affected in some way or another.

It involves difficulties in dealing with the sounds of words which makes it hard to learn the phonics to read words.

For many people with dyslexia, the challenge is not with written words but with short term memory and the speed of processing that are more frustrating than issues with reading and spelling.

In a business environment, dyslexics will be disadvantaged and it is essential that the right support is available so that such difficulties are not seen as a barrier to achievement.

English as a second or other language (ESOL)

The English language is complicated enough at the best of times, even for native English speakers. It is even more of a challenge when English is not your first language, especially when it comes to business writing.

As a non-English business owner getting the words right in contractual documents is vital. When you hear people say 'things have got lost in the translation', that can be very true as in some instances, e.g. Polish, there is sometimes no direct translation so that words or expressions mean the same thing.

Ability / experience of business writing

The ability to write effective business communications is not a God-given gift. For many of us, myself included, it's a skill that is learned over a period of time. The more experience you have the better and more natural it becomes. Having said that, it's not the case for everybody. Some people will always struggle with spelling and grammar for a variety of reasons.

Many years ago, in a previous employment, I went on a course to learn, amongst other things, how to write a business letter – that shows how long ago it was – and I can still remember some of the things I learned and I continue to use those principles today, although more in emails than letters. For example, I was taught never to begin a sentence with the words, 'however' or 'therefore'. Nowadays, it doesn't seem to make any difference but I still uphold my own standards.

I sometimes wonder whether staff nowadays are 'taught' or 'trained' how to write a professional or business-like email. I see many emails where the language used is either wholly inappropriate or is full of basic grammatical and spelling errors. It worries me that business owners and managers may not be aware of the quality of some of the emails emanating from their offices and what they are allowing their staff to send out on behalf of their businesses and what the potential consequences could be.

Time pressure

There are never enough hours in the day to achieve what we want to achieve. The pressures of hitting a deadline can have a dramatic effect on the way we write and the quality of the final product.

Life in the 21st century is being led at such a pace, due mainly to rapid technological advances and the speed and immediacy of social media communications that we can be forgiven for struggling to keep up.

Content is often written, compiled and published in a pressurised environment. If there are many content writers and editors, who all have busy workloads and tight deadlines, it's often the checking process that is foregone and, therefore, it's no wonder that small mistakes can easily slip through the process.

Even when we are encouraged to re-read our own work before pressing the send or print button, time is always the determining factor as to how long is spent checking what we have written. Your eyes and brain will be so familiar with what you have written that it will not pick up simple errors.

This is what I mean:

The mind reads what it expects to see.

The mnid raeds wat it expcets to see.

The mined reeds watt it excepts two sea.

In the second sentence, although the letters in some of the words are jumbled up, you can still read the meaning. In the third sentence, the words are quite obviously incorrect but a spellchecker won't pick any of these up because they are all spelt correctly.

You may be in the habit of re-reading your work several times over. That's fine, but how long is that taking you and how much is it costing you in terms of your time? What else could you have been doing with that time that would be more beneficial to your business? You could consider engaging a proofreader to do the checking for you and to free up that precious time.

Social media influences

The way we write on social media is having a huge influence on the way we write other business communications. With Twitter, for example, we are allowed 140 characters compared with 650 characters on LinkedIn.

These limitations do have an effect on the way we write in general. When the Oxford University Press declared the word *hashtag* as the Children's Word of the Year for 2014, it was revealed that, following the analysis of over 100,000 short stories written by children between the ages of 5 and 13 years old, the use of the hashtag symbol (#) to add extra meaning or comment at the end of the sentence was commonplace.

I know the English language is forever developing and moving forward, but this is an example of just how influential social media is becoming in our lives. As these youngsters, who have not known life without social media, move into the world of business, then maybe we need to keep pace with such changes and adapt our business writing accordingly and appropriately.

Social media is now a big part of the marketing mix and business owners are having to embrace it as a tool to promote and grow their businesses. It is another tool that is also impinging on the time pressures that business owners are already under.

Delegation and outsourcing

The art of delegation is a fine one. Some people find it very difficult to delegate a task to someone else as they feel they are losing control. If you are a sole trader, however, you have no-one to delegate tasks to. This can increase the pressure on solopreneurs as they have to retain responsibility for everything associated with their business regardless of whether they know what they are doing or not.

So, when you don't have the knowledge in house, do you employ someone who has that knowledge or do you engage the services of an external expert?

Outsourcing is where you engage an outside expert or contractor to perform duties on your behalf, e.g. a bookkeeper.

Rather than employing someone and thereby adding the responsibilities of being an employer to your already onerous burden, by engaging a contractor you are only responsible to each other for the task for which they have been engaged.

This may be a one-off task or a series of on-going tasks. They are not your employee and you can terminate the contract at any point, something that brings additional problems if that person had been your employee.

Work / Life balance

This is a perennial challenge for a business owner. Often family demands conflict with business demands and as a result stress levels increase. High stress levels lead to corner-cutting and corner-cutting affects the quality of what you are doing in your business. That applies to business writing too.

If you are writing a report and you are watching the clock because you said you would be home by a certain time, you will inevitably pay less attention to accuracy. You may even send the report off to your client without doing a final check only to discover that key things have been omitted or careless errors have been made.

Let's face it – we've all done it, haven't we? We all know what it's like especially if your client is the one to point out the errors and omissions.

How do these challenges affect business writing?

Business writing is a fundamental part of everything we do in a business. Whether you are a business owner or an employed member of staff, you will write something every day in the normal course of your work that will have an impact on the business.

It could be a simple email to a customer or a supplier; it could be some content for a website; it could be a tender for a big contract or it could be some social media content. No matter what it is, you have to get it right as far as spelling and grammar goes. If that part is flawed then it reflects badly on the quality of your business and the chances of creating a great impression and of attracting and securing new clients.

So in all the above issues facing small business owners there will be a corresponding effect on the quality of the business writing.

Multi-hat wearing

Having to turn your hand to a variety of tasks when running a business, your skills in business writing will be tested to the full.

Whether you are writing formal or informal emails, a business report, a marketing newsletter or website content, what you say and how you say it will vary according to the proposed reader.

If you are a 'jack of all trades and master of none' and you are faced with having to write content for your website, how do you know what you are writing will have the desired effect when it is live on a website? Likewise, you may be writing a formal response to an Invitation to Tender, the style of which is completely different to the 'chattier' style suited for online and social media content.

The challenge, therefore, for a business owner is understanding the difference and being able to adapt your writing style to the medium in question.

Reputation

Having a good reputation in your chosen business is one thing. Building that reputation from scratch is something else. You have to earn that reputation by delivering an excellent product or service, so much so, that people start talking about you and your business and recommending you to their clients. What and how you write as part of your business activity will inevitably contribute to people's judgement and assessment of your abilities. If the standard and quality of your business writing is poor then people will judge you differently than if your style of writing is good.

By producing written material that contains spelling and grammatical errors, your prospective customers will be unlikely to do business with you because the poor quality of your writing will reflect back on the quality of your business. People will think that if you can't be bothered to check what you have written that this will also be the standard of your business.

Having built up your reputation, it's a shame to damage it by producing sub-standard content that contains careless mistakes. The smallest of errors in your content will detract from the impression you are trying to make. Mistakes, no matter how small, convey carelessness which will undermine your hard-earned reputation.

Trying to be good at everything

Very few business owners are good at everything to do with running a business. Not everyone is a skilled writer, however, if it is something you struggle with then it will be noticeable that the quality of what you write may not be as high as you want it to be. You may also think you don't have a problem and it's not until you're notified, maybe by one of your best customers, that your writing contains errors, that you realise it. By that time it could be too late. You could have lost out on a big contract.

There's no shame in admitting that writing is a challenge. That's why there are people out there who can help, so don't be afraid of seeking some expert assistance. It could be the difference between winning and losing that big contract.

Ability to adapt to technological advances

Trying to keep pace with the rapid technological changes that are taking place in the early years of the 21st century is not easy. Neither is it easy to adapt your style of writing so that it has the same impact in a wide variety of media.

The style of writing required to have an impact on social media is very different to a formal business report or a tender response. Having the ability to adapt requires a firm understanding of the differences of style required and being able to write effectively in those styles.

As above, there are people out there who specialise in this sort of thing, so seek them out and use their expertise to your advantage.

Dyslexia/ESOL

Dyslexia affects different people in different ways and at different times in their lives.

Dyslexia is not just a reading problem. Many dyslexics are good readers whilst others will read slowly with inaccuracies. For many, however, having difficulty in dealing with the sounds of words affects the way in which they write and spell those words. Without support, specifically in the workplace, from either internal or external resources, these issues will inevitably affect their business writing and may ultimately affect what is being sent out to potential new or existing customers.

Similar challenges are experienced by people for whom English is their second or other language (ESOL). Being a non-native speaker in any country is a challenge especially when it comes to writing and more so with business writing. As a business owner or as an employee, writing will be an issue that needs to be addressed if you are to succeed with your business.

Ability/experience

Many people of all ages and abilities struggle with spelling and grammar. The English language is complicated at the best of times and for those people who struggle with it, the style and quality of their written work is affected. Young people who leave school with few or no qualifications not only struggle to find work but when they do enter the workplace they are at an immediate disadvantage. They need a high level of support from their employer, which may or may not be available, in order to develop their skills and become confident in their own abilities.

Having basic numeracy and literacy skills are an essential attribute for anyone entering the workplace. Learning how to write in a business context can be a long process particularly if you have no experience. The more you write, however, the better you will become providing helpful feedback is available from supervisors and managers. Being left to sink or swim is not helpful to either the employee or the business otherwise sub-standard communications and publications will be emanating from your business that will have a detrimental effect and potentially damaging consequences.

If, however, you are a sole trader, then you may have that sinking feeling as you will have no-one to check what you are writing and give feedback. You should therefore be seeking the support of a third party, an independent pair of eyes to review what you are writing so that your business is being read about in the best possible light. Don't be afraid to ask a copy writer or a proofreader to help you.

Time pressures

Content is being written these days in a highly pressurised environment. Business owners are keen to get their content out into the public domain quickly in order to maintain or improve their position in the marketplace. Speed can be detrimental and taking just a few minutes to check what you are sending is time well spent.

Busy workloads and tight deadlines mean it's no wonder that small mistakes can easily slip through the process. If your process doesn't include a checking element, i.e. self-checking or by a third party, then your document will be published containing mistakes and it's these mistakes that can come back to bite you when you least expect it.

Mistakes in your written content also infers carelessness. If time is against you to get your content published then your mistakes will be published too. Planning time better to ensure that you have a checking process will significantly improve the effectiveness of your business writing.

Social media

Social media content tends to be written in a hurry either to generate immediate reaction or as a response to a trend. The power and immediacy of social media means that your audience is able to reach far into the blue yonder when it comes to pointing out one of your mistakes. Within seconds, negative feedback is circulating across your network and reaching people who can have a serious effect on your business.

Mobile devices have a habit of incorporating predictive text to messages being sent out over social media. How many times have you been caught out by predictive text? If you press that 'send' button without checking whether your device has changed what you keyed in, then you could be faced with embarrassing and potentially costly consequences. So, just spend a few seconds, preferably more, checking that your intended message is accurate.

Delegation / Outsourcing

The effect on your business writing of delegation or outsourcing is determined by who the task is being delegated or outsourced to. If you delegate a task of compiling a report to a subordinate, you must have confidence in the ability of that person to undertake the task to the level of quality you want. You engage an outsourced person to undertake the task, based on their ability and experience and you will pay them accordingly.

At the end of the day, you get what you pay for. If you have an in-house resource capable of performing the task within the timescale and to the quality required, then why outsource? If that resource is not available or you don't consider they have the time, ability or experience to perform the task, then buy in that expertise either on a one-off basis or on a retainer, if this is to be a regular occurrence. Weighing up the cost-effectiveness of delegating or outsourcing is key to the process.

Consequences of not facing up to these challenges

Whatever challenge is thrown at us, we either confront it head-on or we let it get the better of us.

You're in business to be successful and therefore, I'd suggest you would want to confront a challenge head-on. If you don't, the consequences could be seriously damaging to your business.

When it comes to business writing, the challenges I've highlighted and the effects on your writing all have serious consequences if you don't do something about them.

Any sort of challenge will increase your stress levels and the challenge of business writing is no different. Whether you are dyslexic, a non-native English speaker or someone who just struggles with the written word, your stress levels will inevitably increase. You will get worried about what you are writing or what you have got to write but have been putting off hoping it might go away. It maybe causes you to wake up in the middle of the night. This does happen, believe me, I've been there!!

Writing when you feel stressed out will lead to a poorer quality of the end result. You just want to get the piece finished and out the door so that you can turn your attention to something else a little less stressful. To get a piece of writing finished in this way you will inevitably cut corners in order to save time. This could mean that you don't check what you have written or you don't get someone else to check it for fear of what they may find, you just want to get shot of it. This can lead to a vicious circle because you will then be worried about what you have published and what the potential consequences of that might be. It won't do anything for your stress levels and it will make it worse because when you come to write your next piece, you'll be worrying about previous ones as well as what you should be focussing on.

This is just the scenario when errors are made and missed because the piece isn't being checked and so on until the article or document is published – errors and all.

What I've described here is a real scenario. There are work environments where this happens and the end result is that the reputation of the business and the business owner is damaged, sometimes beyond repair. When you publish an article or send a document to a client that contains errors, your reader - your prospective or existing client - will see the mistakes and they will react accordingly.

They may do nothing. They are more likely, however, to notify you of the mistakes, hopefully for your own good, but how embarrassing is that? They may go even further than that and put a note out on social media – how damaging could that be? They can then cap it all by taking their business elsewhere.

So, you can see just how such a scenario could pan out and when there is so much support and advice available from other agencies, these consequences can be avoided.

Missing a deadline

I come across so many instances where businesses work to deadlines and in most cases everything is left until the last possible moment. There must be something in our genes that says to us, 'don't worry, there's plenty of time....' and when you are a couple of days away from the deadline date you realise just how much still needs to be done and ask yourself, 'why didn't I leave more time?' As a result you end up rushing round like a headless chicken trying to get everything done when a little forethought and planning could have made the whole process that much more straightforward.

Missing a deadline or submitting sub-standard work can have serious consequences for your business. You may lose out on a valuable contract or some much needed funding may be declined, all because you failed to plan the process before and leading up to the deadline date.

I know this happens as I have first-hand experience of writing and submitting such applications against a deadline. I have also been on the other side of the fence as an assessor for funding applications. As an assessor, you have no time to analyse the text in front of you. You have no time to go seeking the information you need to award scores. If you can't read or understand what has been written you have to move on. The result is that you are unable to award the score for that particular section and the knock-on effect is that the overall score for the application will be lower and will, in all likelihood, miss out on the funding being applied for.

Writing a response to a tender invitation or a funding application requires a different style to that of writing social media content, for example.

What is essential, however, is to have a process in place that works backwards from the deadline date so that you can plan what needs to be done, who is going to do it and by when. This process should always include a period for checking what you have written, something that is often discarded because time is against you, the deadline date is looming and you are more concerned about sending it off without being concerned about the quality of what you are sending or the consequences of your application not being successful. Checking that you have at least answered the questions is as important as checking your spelling and grammar.

'We've always done it this way'

So often I hear people say, 'but we've always done it this way'. It may be that the reason it has always been done that way is because other ways have been tried and proven ineffective – or have they?

Maybe things have always been done that way because nothing different has been tried and no-one has ever raised the question. We tend to protect ourselves from the fear of the unknown and shy away from anything that upsets the status quo.

Is change a good thing? Change needs to be for a reason. Often great ideas come from the employees who can spot better ways of doing things.

In some cases, continuing to do what you've always done is perfectly reasonable, no change is needed; what's important is having the ability to recognise and speak up when something doesn't feel quite right or doesn't appear to be working any more.

It may be that there's something about the way you do your business writing that frustrates you. You may be so used to writing something and then checking it yourself, maybe several times over, before you are satisfied it's right and then sending it off without even thinking of the consequences of your actions. Just because that's what you've always done, it doesn't mean that there isn't a more time/cost-effective way of doing it.

In this scenario, it's good that the work is being checked but should you be checking your own work?

If that's what you've always done, that's fine, but let's look at another consequence of you doing that. When you check your own writing, your eyes and brain will be so familiar with the text, that they will see what's written but not notice that what's written may not necessarily be right. An independent pair of eyes, however, won't have read that text before and therefore will be able to pick up any errors that much more quickly.

Also, take the length of time spent reading and re-reading your writing and then put a cost against that time. Take your hourly or daily rate and multiply it by the time spent and you will get a true value of what you have spent. If this is repeated on numerous occasions because you've always done that, then it all adds up.

Think also about what else you could have been doing with that time. I'm sure there are more cost-effective activities relating to your business that you could have been doing. That's why working with a proofreader not only gives you that time back but you will be able to use that time to better advantage.

How easy it is to make mistakes

We all make mistakes. It's a fact of life. We usually pick ourselves up, dust ourselves down and move on.

Every once in a while though, a mistake we've made will come back to bite us when we least expect it and sometimes it can prove quite costly.

Imagine for a minute that you are a top goalkeeper. You'll make thousands of saves in your career but you will let a few through. Just suppose the ones you let through are in key games like an FA Cup Final and you end up on the losing side, you're going to feel gutted. So will your team-mates.

If we put this analogy into a business context and suppose that your errors have cost your business a lucrative new contract which has now gone to one of your competitors, again, you're going to be feeling pretty gutted, as will your work colleagues.

Making these sorts of mistakes in your business writing can be costly but by taking a bit of extra care we can eradicate some, if not all, of these errors.

Here are a few examples of common errors that I come across whilst proofreading, all of which can easily be avoided:

Words with additional letters

It's very easy to add a letter by mistake and it's equally as easy to miss them when you are reading it back quickly, e.g.

illlicit,   acccountant

Words with missing letters

Again, it's just as easy to miss a letter out, e.g.

acommodation or accomodation (correct spelling – accommodation)

embarass or embarras (correct spelling – embarrass)

comittee or commitee (correct spelling – committee)

In both of the above examples, the errors should be picked up by Word's Auto-Correct function and show a red squiggly line under the word but if you haven't got that switched on then they may slip through, and you will be amazed at how many do just that!

If you've written this and you're reading it back, your eyes and your brain will be unlikely to spot the mistakes because they are familiar with what has been written. If an independent pair of eyes reads it, then they are much more likely to spot the error because the text is unfamiliar.

Words that are correct, yet incorrect

There are lots of words that are spelt correctly even though you may have transposed a letter or just typed it incorrectly, e.g.

casual or causal

nuclear or unclear

form or from

than or that

nor or not or now

When you read these words quickly your eyes will recognise the word as being correct but may not register the fact that it's wrong. Word's Auto-Correct won't highlight them as they are spelt correctly and your spellchecker will probably not pick them up either.

Words which sound the same but have different meanings

There must be hundreds of occasions when you've thought twice over a word that you've typed and asked the question, 'Is that right?' How many times, though, have you actually referred to a dictionary or a thesaurus to check it out or just thought, 'Blow it, let it go...'

Well, here are 21 examples of pairs of words that can fit into that category of making you think twice and that cause people so many problems if they don't and end up getting them the wrong way round.

Adverse / Averse
> *Adverse* means 'harmful or unfavourable' whereas...
> *Averse* means 'having a strong dislike to...'

Advice / Advise
> *Advice* means 'guidance with regard to a future action' whereas...
> *Advise* is the verb to give guidance or advice to.

Affect / Effect
> *Affect* means 'to alter or influence' or 'to have an *effect* on something' whereas...
> *Effect* means 'a result' or 'to make something happen'.

Compliment / Complement
> *Compliment* is an 'expression of praise or admiration' whereas...
> *Complement* means 'something that adds value to...'

Criterion / Criteria
> *Criterion* is the singular of criteria – a basis for comparison, whereas...
> *Criteria,* the plural of criterion, means 'one or more bases for comparison'.

Discreet / Discrete
> *Discreet* means 'careful and prudent' whereas...
> *Discrete* means 'separate and distinct'.

Elicit / Illicit
> *Elicit* means 'to evoke or draw out' whereas...

Illicit means 'illegal or unlawful'.

Farther / Further
> *Farther* tends to be used to infer 'a great distance away' whereas...
> *Further* can mean 'moreover' as well as 'to promote or advance a theory'.

Formally / Formerly
> *Formally* means 'officially' whereas...
> *Formerly* means 'in the past or latterly'.

i.e. / e.g.
> *i.e. (id est)* means 'that is' or 'in other words' whereas...
> *e.g. (exempli gratia)* means 'for example'

Imply / Infer
> *Imply* means 'to suggest' whereas...
> *Infer* means 'to deduce from evidence and reasoning'.

Insure / Ensure
> *Insure* means 'to secure or protect against damage' whereas...
> *Ensure* means 'to make certain that something will happen'.

It's / Its
> *It's* is short for 'it is' whereas...
> *Its* is the possessive form of 'it'.

Loathe / Loath
> *Loathe* means 'to hate or detest' whereas...
> *Loath* means 'reluctant or unwilling'

Number / Amount
> *Number* is used 'to count, measure or label something' whereas...
> *Amount* is the 'total collection in size or extent'.

Precede / Proceed
> *Precede* means 'to come before something in time' whereas...
> *Proceed* means 'to begin a course of action' or 'to move forward'.

Principal / Principle
> *Principal* means 'first in order of importance' whereas...
> *Principle* means 'a fundamental rule of conduct'.

They're / Their
> *They're* is short for 'they are' whereas...
> *Their* is the possessive of 'they'.

Who / That
> *Who* is used when referring to a person whereas...
> *That* is used when referring to an object or thing

Who's / Whose
> *Who's* is short for 'who is' whereas...
> *Whose* is the possessive form of 'who'.

You're / Your
> *You're* is short for 'you are' whereas...
> *Your* is the possessive form of 'you'.

Definitions and meanings courtesy of *The New Oxford Dictionary for Writers and Editors*

Again, even though these words have been spelt correctly, your Auto-Correct or spellchecker may not pick them up.

The Business Writing Process Plan

Business writing is something we do every day and as we have seen in the previous chapters for many it is something we just take for granted. For others, however, it causes some issues that can have knock-on consequences for themselves and their businesses.

I believe also in many cases that business owners do not have a process in place that could help alleviate some of these issues. I believe it's because we just take the subject for granted. It's something we do without thinking because we've always done it so why bother with a process? Subconsciously, we may be going through a process but we're not aware of it. The attitude is often, 'Let's do it, let's just write it and get rid of it' without thinking twice about any consequences.

Using a project management mentality where everything is process driven towards a successful outcome, I believe business writing falls into that category too. It may be that you have a process you adhere to but you don't realise it. You just do it. You haven't got anything written down. You haven't got a set of tick boxes so you can monitor your progress.

I think there is a case for writing it down so that it can help people who do struggle with their writing and to help them to overcome their anxieties and so help to get their writing right.

The Business Writing Process Plan (BWPP) is a simple 7-step process that can be used for any document that you are writing, from something as short as an email to be used in a marketing campaign to a substantial document like a response to an Invitation to Tender.

The Business Writing Process Plan (BWPP)

Step 1 Identify what you are writing

Step 2 Ascertain Deadline Date

Step 3 Develop Plan (including some contingency time)
- o   Ascertain tasks that contribute to writing.
- o   Identify other contributors and agree roles and responsibilities and agree an interim deadline for their contributions.
- o   Critical Path Analysis.
- o   Set up other interim deadline dates.

Step 4 Create Content

Step 5 Checking Process

Step 6 Publication Process

Step 7 Feedback monitoring and Reporting

The BWPP is a process that can dovetail with your Content Strategy – if you've got one!

What is a Content Strategy?

Without a content strategy you are likely to either be missing commercial opportunities or be wasting resources on creating and publishing material which fails to serve a useful purpose.

The main elements of a Content Strategy are:

1. Objectives (= BWPP Step 1)
   a. What do you want to achieve through writing and publishing your content?

2. Planning (= BWPP Steps 2 & 3)
   a. What content should be used where and why?

3. Creating content (= BWPP Steps 4 & 5)
   a. What tone and voice will be used to reflect your business and appeal to your customers?
   b. Does your business have a house style?
   c. Will content be written in-house or outsourced to a contracted expert?

4. Publishing content (=BWPP Step 6)
   a. Define publishing
   b. Sending content to a client, e.g. a business report
   c. Submission of a tender or funding application to a funding sponsor
   d. Publication of content online on a website or social media platform

5. Maintenance and Evaluation of content (=BWPP Step 7)
   a. Does the content need to be updated?

   b. Can it be replicated across other media platforms?

   c. Assessing the effectiveness of the content and whether you have achieved your objectives cost-effectively

How does BWPP dovetail with a Content Strategy?

Content Strategy - Objectives
BWPP Step 1: Identify what you are writing
Everything you write in your business has a purpose, otherwise why are you writing it? You're writing it to achieve something. For example:

1. You may be responding to a request for information about your product or service. With your response you will want to impress your prospective client so that they do business with you.
2. You may be writing a formal business report for a client based on work that you've carried out. You will want your report to be as comprehensive as possible and contain all the information in a format that is easily understood and that your client requires.
3. You may be writing marketing content in the form of a newsletter, a flyer, a blog post etc. In each of these you will want to show your business in the best possible light to attract new clients.

The list is endless but with every piece of writing consider why you are writing it and what you want to achieve by writing it.

By focussing on what you want to achieve, this may well influence what you write and the style in which you write it. Consider the intended recipient or reader. What are they going to think about it and will they take the action you want them to take?

Content Strategy - Planning
BWPP Step 2: Ascertain Deadline Date

Do you have a deadline by which whatever you are writing has to be finished by, submitted or published? A deadline could be within an hour; by the end of the day; by the end of next week and so on. This often contributes to many of the issues faced by business owners when they are writing something, including increased stress levels.

If you have a deadline you need to be fully aware of it. By working backwards from that date or time you will know how long you have got to write your piece and you can develop a simple plan of when it can be written.

BWPP Step 3: Develop Your Plan

Developing a plan will enable you to identify the precise tasks involved in writing your piece. Always build in some contingency time here and there because something will always go wrong when you least expect it, so having some additional time will help to alleviate this. If you don't end up using this contingency time, that's great, but you would have regretted it if you needed it and it wasn't there. Such tasks can include:

1. Research – gathering together all the necessary information you are going to need.

2. Identifying who will be responsible for writing the piece.
   As discussed already, an issue for a business

owner when faced with a writing task is having the necessary time, knowledge and expertise to carry out the task. This can often lead to increased stress levels when the task can easily be delegated to other people either in-house, if you have them and they have all the necessary attributes, or, if not, to an outside expert like a copy writer.

3. Don't forget that you will need to brief the copy writer and allow time for that copy writer to undertake research of their own so that they fully understand your business and the tone of what you require to be written.

4. Establishing roles and responsibilities. Agreeing who will write what and by when they need to submit it to you for inclusion in the final piece.

5. Knowing the final deadline date will enable you to set an interim deadline for submission of material to you.

6. Critical Path Analysis
This is a well-known planning tool that can help you to establish which tasks can be done simultaneously and which tasks rely on other tasks being completed first.

7. Where will you write?
Do you need to book a quiet space in your office so you are away from any distractions, e.g. telephone, computer with emails and social media.

Content Strategy – Creating Content
BWPP Step 4: Create content

This is the step where you actually start writing. Steps 1-3 may be very quick if you are doing all the planning and the writing yourself. Having ascertained what you are writing and why, you should then determine the tone and voice of your writing. This will depend on your intended reader. It will reflect back on your business and will determine your appeal to your clients. It will also be determined by the intended media through which it will be published.

You will have a different tone and voice for a formal report or tender compared to social media and website content.

You will also have determined whether you are doing the writing yourself or whether you have engaged an external copy writer.

Another thing to consider is whether your business has a house style. What I mean by a house style is that everyone in your business is using a consistent style and layout so that from the outside it appears as though you are a professional looking outfit. Even if you're a sole trader, you will need to make sure that everything you publish is consistent in its format and layout.

All major corporates have their own brand identity and house styles, so why not a small business too? I will look at how you can develop your own house style later in the book.

BWPP Step 5: Checking Process

From my experience as a proofreader, this step is more often than not the one that is overlooked and is probably as important, if not more important, than all the other steps in the process.

One reason that it's overlooked is because you haven't factored in enough time to do it before the deadline looms or you have just given your work a cursory glance before hitting the 'print' or 'send' buttons and then maybe regretting it at a later date. This is how mistakes are missed and a sub-standard piece of writing is published with sometimes costly consequences.

By factoring in time for checking you'll be able to edit or re-write some of what you've written so that it reads better. Copy editing done properly is a skill and is not the same as proofreading.

Through the editing process you, or an experienced copy editor, have an opportunity to change what has been written, to add or delete text, to move it around and to make the overall feel and appearance of the document look better.

A proofreader, on the other hand, will check for spelling, grammar and punctuation errors, as well as looking at the consistency in the text and the layout. By consistency, I mean, for example, that a word or name used throughout the text is spelt correctly and used in the right context each time. For layout, for example, where headings and footers are used they should be positioned correctly and consistently throughout the document where relevant.

The purpose of the checking process is to ensure that your writing is accurate, free from errors and looks professional. At the end of the day no matter what you're writing, whether it's a letter, a business report, a newsletter, marketing material or social media content, it will either be directly promoting your business or it will be reflecting back on the quality of your business. What better reason for getting it right and giving you that chance to create a great impression with your existing and prospective clients and to protect your hard-earned reputation.

Content Strategy – Publication Process
BWPP Step 6: Publication

There are many different ways of publishing a piece of writing. When you publish something, the article or document in question is leaving your business and is being sent to someone else, maybe a client, or maybe it's entering the public domain. Other people will be able to read it, both intended and unintended. Those people will be in a position to make a judgement about you and your business should they so choose.

Some people make a judgement about a business by its website, its printed literature or other written content. Some, but not all, will refuse to do business with you if they see a spelling or grammatical error on your website. They may think, 'Why should I place my trust in a business that can't be bothered to check what they post on their website?' It's careless and reflects badly on the business.

You will already have determined, through your plan, how your publication is to be distributed. You may need to get it professionally printed in which case you should have factored in time for a printer to set up your document, produce a proof for you to verify and approve (don't forget, printers are not proofreaders) before they press the 'print' button – the point of no return if you have missed an error.

I have seen so many examples of printed material that contain errors that have then been destroyed and re-printed. Not only is it a waste of time, paper and printer ink, it is a very costly exercise too.

Electronic distribution is even more scary because once you have pressed the 'send' button you haven't got a point of no return. It's gone out into the ether and will be open to all sorts of scrutiny and comment, some welcome and some not.

If you have been diligent with your checking you should have fewer worries than if you haven't.

Content Strategy – Maintenance and Evaluation
BWPP Step 7: Feedback monitoring and reporting

Receiving feedback, both positive and negative, as a direct result of something you've written, is exceedingly valuable. If nothing else, it means that someone has actually taken the time and trouble to read what you've written and to make comment.

In some cases you'll be able to put a realistic value on the feedback if you go on to sign up a new client. Feedback to a newsletter will enable you to make changes next time, if appropriate. If you have had a tender or a funding application declined, then feedback obtained will enable you to learn lessons for the next occasion.

Some of your content can be re-cycled, maybe as a blog post with accompanying social media posts and links. The original text may have to be tweaked a bit to have the desired effect in a different medium.

Your feedback will also enable you to evaluate whether a piece of writing has been worthwhile, e.g. has it brought in any new business? Has it raised awareness of your business and, in general, have you achieved your objectives?

You may feel that this whole process is going over the top but no matter what you're writing you can apply the process. In many instances, it can be a quick 'yes' or 'no' answer to each step but at least you will have been through the process consciously rather than subconsciously.

Here are a few scenarios in which the BWPP can be used:

Scenario 1 - Newsletter

Identify what are you writing?
Newsletter
Why? To publicise activities and up-coming events
Achieve? To notify members of activities and events

Ascertain Deadline Date
Newsletter published quarterly
1st February; 1st May; 1st August; 1st November

Develop Plan
Today = 10th May
Next Deadline = 31st July for 1st August

Ascertain tasks that contribute to writing
Gather together news articles, ideas and information
Agree who is writing which articles; will it be written
in-house or by an outside agency?
Set interim deadline for all contributions and images
(30th June)

Critical Path Analysis
Contributors can write articles simultaneously -
submit to editor by 30th June
Layout planning will have to wait until all articles
received (10th July)

Set interim deadlines
Prepare newsletter for proofreader (17th July)
Receive newsletter back from proofreader (20th July)
Send to printer (21st July)
Receive proof from printer for approval (23rd July)
Receive print copies from printer (27th July)
Publish 1st August

Write Content
Contributors to write content and submit to editor by
30th June
Images to be sourced and submitted by 30th June

Checking Process
Editor to compile draft newsletter ready to be sent to
proofreader by 17th July
Receive proofreader's amendments and comments by
20th July
Act on proofreader's comments by 21st July

Publication Process
Prepare and send copy to printers by 21st July
Receive a proof from printers for final approval by 23rd
July
Finished newsletters received from printers by 27th
July
Publish 1st August

Feedback monitoring & Reporting
Review process and learn lessons for next newsletter
Receive feedback from newsletter readers and act
accordingly

Scenario 2 - Response to Invitation to Tender or Funding Application

Identify what you are writing
Response to Invitation to Tender or Funding
Application
Why? To secure new contract or funding
Achieve? To enable new project to proceed

Ascertain Deadline Date
The ITT and Funding Call will have a deadline date
(and time) by which applications must be received.
Work out the final date by which your application
must be posted (for hard copy applications) to reach
funding sponsors before the deadline. For electronic
submissions, be aware that the online system will be
very busy leading up to the deadline so work out your
final submission date and time well in advance so as
not to get caught out should the system crash.

Develop Plan
Today = D-Day -20

Ascertain tasks that contribute to writing
Ascertain who is responsible for submitting tender =
Bid Manager (D-20)
Engage outsourced expert, if appropriate and agree
role (D-20)
Ascertain and agree what information is needed and
who will provide it (D-20)
Set a date for that information to be submitted to Bid
Manager (D-15)

Critical Path Analysis
Standard organisational information can be prepared
at the same time as specific tender information is
being gathered.

Liaison with financial team can be done now in anticipation of preparing budgets.

Set interim deadlines
Tender writing completion (D-10)
Checking and sign-off (D-5)
Compilation of final submission (D-3)
Submission by Registered Mail (D-2)
Confirm receipt by funding sponsor (D-1/D-0)

Create Content
Make sure you are clear about the questions to be answered.
Write content within word/character restrictions - in-house or contractor?

Checking Process
Bid Manager to get content checked by proofreader/ appraiser.
Check for spelling and grammar.
Check that content written answers the questions.
Check for word/character count.
Obtain final sign-off.

Publication Process
Gather together hard copies of all necessary content for submission.
Make sure required number of copies has been made.
Send by Registered Mail to Funding Sponsor (D-2) to ensure it arrives well in time prior to D-Day.

Feedback monitoring and Reporting
Confirm submission has been received by Funding Sponsor.
Review tender submission process and learn any lessons for the next submission.
Await response from Funding Sponsor.

Scenario 3 - Website Content

Identify what you are writing
Website Content (including blogs)
Why? To promote new service
Achieve? Increased sales

Ascertain Deadline Date
Website (re)launch date = D-10

Develop Plan
Agree who will write the content - in-house or external copy/content writer?
Agree date by which content will be written (D-5).

Critical Path Analysis
Web designer can be building site (if new site) and sourcing images whilst content is being written.
Arrange and record video, if appropriate.
Engage help, if required, for SEO.

Create Content
Be aware of the style of writing required for website content.

Checking Process
Arrange for content to be proofread for spelling, grammar and consistency across the site (D-4).
Act on proofreader's amendments and comments (D-2).

Publication Process
Arrange for content, images, videos, hyperlinks etc. to be uploaded to site (D-1).
Launch site on agreed date (D-0).
Publicise across social media and elsewhere, as

appropriate.

Feedback monitoring and Reporting
Ascertain comments from clients.
Check SEO analysis.

Scenario 4 - Social Media Content

Ascertain what you are writing
Regular content to be scheduled on social media platforms.
Why? As part of market mix to promote business
Achieve? Increased traffic to website

Ascertain Deadline Date
Refer to your Social Media Strategy.
One day per month spent scheduling social media content on whatever platform(s) are most appropriate to your business.

Develop Plan
Today is D-7.

Ascertain tasks that contribute to writing
Agree which platforms will be used, e.g. Twitter, Facebook etc. (D-7).
Agree key themes and keywords/phrases (D-6).
Engage external copy/content writer, if appropriate (D-6).

Critical Path Analysis
May not be applicable.

Set interim deadlines
Agree when content must be ready before scheduling

(D-4).
Arrange for content to be proofread and checked for spelling, grammar and consistency of message across various platforms (D-4).

Create Content
Use appropriate writing style for platform and keep within character limitations.

Checking Process
Arrange for content to be sent to proofreader to check for spelling, grammar and consistency of message across the various platforms (D-3).
Act on proofreader's amendments and comments (D-2).

Publication Process
Schedule posts using appropriate intermediary, e.g. Hootsuite.

Feedback monitoring and Reporting
Monitor reach of posts through appropriate intermediaries, e.g. Tweriod, Google Analytics etc.

What else could you do?

Change the way you do things

Have you ever looked at the way you do things within your business? Have you ever asked the question, 'Why do we do it this way?' Do you come up with the answer, 'Because we've always done it this way'?

Could it be that no-one has ever actually asked the question and you've blindly continued along the same path? Well, ask yourself that question now and have a look at some of your processes.

As this book is about business writing and in the previous chapter I introduced you to the Business Writing Process Plan (BWPP), could you use the BWPP in your business, or just part of it? You may be doing it subconsciously already. How about doing it consciously? Actually think about what you are writing and why you are writing it. What are you hoping to achieve by writing it?

OK, it may take you a bit longer but at the same time, by thinking about it, it may lead you to changing the way you do things, making it more cost-effective in the long run. Then you'll say to yourself, 'Why didn't we do this earlier?'

Let me throw in a couple of real scenarios:

Pizza Express

Every morning when staff arrived for their shift at Pizza Express, one waiter would slice the lemons ready to garnish the drinks throughout the day. The job involved them cleaning an area to prepare the lemons, chopping them and then cleaning up afterwards.

One pizza chef then suggested it might be easier for his team to do it instead. Considering they were spending most of their morning chopping and preparing ingredients for the pizza and pasta dishes, it made a lot of sense. The chefs already had all the tools to hand and did not need to clear a space, or clean up, until after their shift had finished, therefore saving considerable valuable time.

Swan Vesta

A factory worker made a simple recommendation. By putting sandpaper used to strike the matches on only one side of the matchbox instead of both, it saved the company millions of pounds.

Outsourcing

Now that you are consciously thinking about how and why you do the things the way you do, maybe now is the time to think about how you could do these things differently.

Do you try and do everything in-house? Are you and your staff rushed off your feet trying to get everything done and, as a result, you're cutting corners and compromising on the quality of your end product? Well, maybe a change is what you need to consider.

As a business owner you may be great at delegating tasks to other people within your business. If so, you obviously have great faith in their abilities to undertake the task, but do they actually have the ability and also the time to do it properly and to the standard that you expect? Do you then have to check what they've done to make sure that they've done what you asked them to do? How much time does that take and how much does all that time cost?

This may be the issue. There are people out there who not only have the ability and expertise but they also have the time to devote to your business.

What is outsourcing?

If you don't have the in-house resource or expertise, one option is to consider outsourcing some of your work to one of a growing band of freelancers or consultants who are happy to work on a temporary or part-time basis, often bringing specialist skills and expertise with them. You can work with them on a one-off piece of work or as many as you choose. You are in control and you bring them in as and when you need them. It also means that you don't have to employ someone and then have all the additional issues that go with PAYE and other employment matters.

What should you outsource?

Ask yourself another question, 'What am I good at?' or 'Where are my (and my team's) skills best utilised?'

If you are great at sales and marketing and not so hot on admin and finance, then you could consider getting some outside help and work with a virtual PA or a bookkeeper.

Outsourcing a routine function such as admin or bookkeeping, could free up time that you need to spend on delivering your product or service.

These are all key business processes, just as your business writing is a key process but something you may always have taken for granted as something you just do, without thinking about the consequences of compromising on the quality of your output.

Now that you are thinking about your business writing processes consciously and maybe you're going to start using the BWPP, then you may want to look at outsourcing some of your written work to specialist freelancers.

Business Writing Specialists

Whether you struggle with your business writing or not, as highlighted in the previous chapters, time may be your biggest issue, or a lack of it. This is when a business writing specialist can really help.

Copy/Content Writers

By consciously thinking about what and why you are writing and what you aim to achieve as a result, it may be that you realise you don't actually have the skills, or the time, you thought you had in order to be able to do a great job.

Copy, or content, writers have the skill and expertise to turn your business issue into the style of writing most appropriate for your situation. They will probably take a fraction of the time that you and your staff would spend on it and as a result the cost of such an expert will probably be a fraction of the cost that you and your staff would have incurred. This is where outsourcing comes into its own because not only are you saving time and money but you are also getting back the time to spend on other business related activities.

Copy Editors

Let's suppose you are writing a book all about your business or something specific relating to your business.

It's obvious that you are the best person to write the book because you know your subject better than anyone else.

So, you embark upon the task and eventually you have written 75,000 words. Fantastic. Well done! You're probably wiping your brow with relief and can't wait to get it published and earning some money.

Whoa! Slow down! You're nowhere near the publishing stage yet.

The first thing you must do is edit what you've written. You will have been so engrossed and focussed on what you have written that you've probably repeated various parts of the book more than once. It's also possible that chapters or sections are in the wrong order and the book doesn't flow properly. You may also need a contents section or even an index. Now that is a skilled job to put an index in place.

Unless you've got people in-house that know what they're doing, you'll need to engage a skilled copy editor.

A copy editor will read your manuscript and work with you to get everything in the right order, layout and context, so that when your hoped-for thousands of customers read your book they will be moved by it to take the action you want them to take.

In the world of book publishing, the copy editor is the glue between you, the author, and the reader and is responsible for making sure that your manuscript ends up looking and reading as well as possible.

Proofreaders

The other key component to publishing not only a book but also any other document that directly promotes or reflects back on the quality of your business, is a proofreader.

Whether you have employed a copy writer and/or editor or not, it is essential that whatever you have written is checked, ideally by an 'independent pair of eyes'.

Statistics from a recent survey showed that over 60% of respondents seeing mistakes in marketing literature or website content would not do business with those organisations. They said, 'If they can't be bothered to check what they have written then why should I place my trust in them to do a good job for me?'

A proofreader will check for more than spelling and grammatical errors. He/she will look at the way a document is laid out as well as checking for consistency of context across a document or website.

Again, whilst you've been engrossed and focussed on what you've been writing, a proofreader, reading a piece for the first time, will cast an independent pair of eyes over what you've written. Any errors will be much more apparent much more quickly than if you were to proofread your own writing. That's because your eyes and brain are so familiar with what is on the page or the screen, they won't notice the smallest of errors. It's these small errors that are often missed and come back to bite you further down the line.

As with a copy writer and editor, a proofreader can free up your time to do other things within your business.

House styles

As a proofreader, as well as looking for spelling and grammatical errors, I also look at the way a document is laid out and the consistency of the style used. What does this mean?

As a business, do you have your own 'house style'? In other words, is everyone in your business using a consistent style and layout so that from the outside it appears as though you're a professional looking organisation?

You'll have noticed that all major corporates have their own identity and style when communicating. It's no different for a smaller business. Having your own corporate identity or house style is just as important if you are going to create that all important GREAT first impression.

A house style for a small business doesn't have to be as complex as that of a major corporate, in fact, the simpler the better, so that everyone understands what they have to do to be consistent in their approach when communicating on behalf of the business.

Whatever decisions you make regarding your own house style, make sure they are written down as a company policy and circulated to all staff so that they know what is required of them.

Here are a few tips on what to think about when designing your own house style:

Company/Business Name and Logo

These are the most individual things that your business has to identify itself, so it is vital that they appear – in the same format – on all your letterheads, compliments slips, business cards, invoices, newsletters etc.

All emails emanating from your business should have the logo, address and contact details of the individual sending it. Don't forget to include, in the small print at the foot of your emails, your business registration information including the registered address.

Fonts

There are hundreds of fonts to choose from but it's important that whichever one you opt for, you use across the whole company.

Some fonts are called *sans serif*, such as Arial or Verdana. This sentence is written in Arial and there are no twiddly bits on the ends of characters.

Serif fonts, on the other hand, do have the twiddly bits. This book is written in Century Schoolbook so you should be able to tell the difference. Which would you prefer for your business?

Bullet Points and Numbered Lists

Again, there are many styles to choose from and whichever you choose must become standard across the organisation
* You can have the traditional bullet point like this one
   * Or a more unusual one

With numbered lists, again there are a variety of styles to choose from, e.g.
1. Simple numbers like this one
    1.1. Or multi-level lists like this
    1.2. And so on....

If your bulleted/numbered text is a complete sentence it should end in a full stop, whereas if the bullets/numbers are just a list of words/phrases, then each should be followed by a semi-colon or left blank.

Headings

Make sure that all your headings are consistent in terms of font, style (upper/lower case) and positioning (left/centred/right).

Choose also if you are going to have the same heading throughout a document, i.e. the document title on every page or the document title on one page and maybe the chapter/section heading on the facing page. Whichever you choose, be consistent throughout the whole document.

Footers

The most common theme to have in the footer space is page numbers. As with the heading, make sure they are consistent in terms of style (words or numerals) and positioning (left/centred/right).

You may want to have your website URL as part of your footer. Consider whether you include the www. prefix or not and then be consistent with whichever format you choose.

Margins

The space on the page around your text is very important. If you have a very narrow margin your text will appear very close to the edge of the page. Consequently, a full page of text in this style will be much more challenging to read than a page where the margins are wide and the line spacing is clear.

Numerals

There is always a lot of debate about whether numerals should be written in words or in number format. There are no rules and you do whatever you want to do. A common format is to have *one* to *ten* written in words and *11* onwards written in number format, but you choose whichever format looks best for your organisation and be consistent.

If you use tables or images a lot then each item will invariably have a caption to describe it. Often those captions are numbered, e.g. Table 1, Table 2 or 1.1, 1.2, 1.3 or 1.1, 1.11, 1.12... Again, you choose what works best for your business and stick to it.

Other decisions to make include the style of numerals you want to use, such as:
Thousands, millions etc.
1,000 or 1000 or 1k;
1,000,000 or 1000000 or 1million or 1m;

First, second, third etc.
In full or 1st, 2nd, 3rd;

Decimals and fractions
0.25 or ¼

Percentages
10 per cent or 10%

Dates
1 March 2015 or 1st March 2015 or March 1st 2015;
1/3/15 or 1/3/2015 or 1.3.2015;

Times
9.30pm or 21.30

Abbreviations and Acronyms

In many instances you will want to use an abbreviation instead of writing out the words in full, for example (or e.g.) and whether to use full stops:

a.m. or am
p.m. or pm
e.g. or eg
i.e. or ie

The general rule for acronyms is that a full stop should not be used between letters, such as BBC, UK, USA, etc. Those that can be pronounced as words, such as Unicef, should be written in lower case with an initial capital letter.

Abbreviations and acronyms are now commonplace in social media language and such shortened versions are now becoming much more prevalent in longer forms of writing. Where you are using an abbreviation for the first time in a piece of text, it should be written out in full with the abbreviation/acronym following in brackets.

Punctuation

If, like me, you have read *"Eats, Shoots and Leaves"* by Lynn Truss, you will have a keen interest in the correct use of punctuation. It seems to me that maybe it's a generational thing as the (correct) use of punctuation seems to be being overlooked throughout our education system. I've seen some horrendous pieces of writing recently that have been completely devoid of any punctuation marks, apart from the full stop at the ends of the sentences.

Let's have a look at some examples of commonly used punctuation marks that cause us so many problems.........

Apostrophes

I don't know about you but it really bugs me when I see an apostrophe being used incorrectly. It's such an insignificant little mark you probably don't even notice it when you're reading at normal speed....

....and that's the nub of the issue. People either don't notice it's there (or not) or they don't notice whether it's correct (or not), but I **do** notice it!

Why not become a member of the Apostrophe Protection Society (www.apostrophe.org.uk).

So, how should an apostrophe be used?

Firstly, it's used to show that something belongs to someone, e.g.

Singular nouns and personal names:
The dog's tail – says that the tail belongs to the dog.
John's car – says that the car belongs to John.

Personal names that end in –s:
Charles's ball – says that the ball belongs to Charles
BUT some place names are an exception to this rule, such as:
St Thomas' Hospital
BUT St James's Palace is an exception to that rule.
How confusing is that?

Plural nouns that end in –s:
The dogs' bowls – says that the bowls belong to some dogs.
Employees' workplace – says that the workplace belongs to the employees.

Plural nouns not ending in –s:
The men's hats – says that the hats belong to the men.
The children's toys – says that the toys belong to the children.
The women's coats – says the coats belong to the women.

Secondly, it's used to show that letters have been left out, e.g.

I'm – is short for 'I am'
They're – is short for 'they are'
Didn't – is short for 'did not'
He'll – is short for 'he will'
It's – is short for 'it is' or 'it has'

The apostrophe goes where the letters have been missed out and is used this way in **informal** writing. You should not shorten words when you are writing formal letters or emails.

Comma

The comma is being used less and less nowadays as we become slaves to social media. There's a time and place for that kind of communication but there should always be a place for the humble little comma, especially in longer forms of writing.

If you've written a long sentence, a comma should be used to denote a natural pause, to make it easier to understand the full context of the sentence. Sometimes we write long lists of items and each item should be separated by a comma. The perennial debate surrounding the serial comma (or the Oxford comma) goes on, i.e. using it in a list before the word 'and'. On the whole, I'm in favour of it.

Semi-colon

Think of the semi-colon as the big brother of the comma. It should be used to separate long phrases in a list or to link two or more related clauses that would otherwise be joined by 'and' or 'but'.

Colon

The colon is most commonly used to introduce a list such as this:
   a. It could be used to introduce a series of bullet points or
   b. A numbered list

Dashes and hyphens

Instead of using commas or semi-colons, we sometimes use dashes which should not be confused with hyphens. This gets a bit more complicated depending on which side of the Pond you are.

The en-rule dash (–) tends to be used in British styles (in MS Word the short-cut is Ctrl1) and the em-rule dash (—) tends to be used in American styles (in MS Word the short-cut is Ctrl2). You can see that the em-rule dash is slightly longer than the en-rule dash and they are both longer than a hyphen.

Dashes can be used to explain something instead of using a comma or brackets, e.g. *'the coat – with its 4 pockets – is very popular with walkers'* or to show a sequence, e.g. *2013–2014, A–Z, London–Brighton.*

A hyphen (-), on the other hand, is not the same as an en-rule dash (–). It's half the length for a start.

A *soft hyphen* is inserted automatically by your word processing software when there isn't enough room on the line. It will disappear if you move the text around. Then there is a *hard hyphen* which is inserted when you consciously key the mark to divide a word in two. It will stay there when you move text around.

There are some words that can be a bit misleading when they are split by a hyphen at the end of a line, e.g.

First part	*Good*	*Misleading*
Dec-	laration	ision
Desig-	nate	ners
Mac-	intosh	hine
Mean-	ing	der
Read-	ing	just
Rein-	deer	force
Thou-	sands	ghtful

There are some other word breaks that need particular care as they could get you into some bother if they go un-noticed, e.g.

Mans- laughter
The- rapist
Mole- sting

Full stop or Full point

Last but by no means least, the full stop or the full point is used to denote the end of a sentence, unless you are using an exclamation mark or a question mark to achieve the same purpose.

A famous example of how well to use a full stop came in a book entitled: *1066 and All That*, which was a spoof History of England and the final sentence simply read: "America became 'top nation', and history came to a."

Appendix 1

Business Writing Process Plan (BWPP)

Step 1: Identify what you are writing *Why are you writing it?* *What do you want to achieve by writing it?*
Step 2: Ascertain Deadline Date/ Time *What is today's date/time?* *How long do you have to complete your writing?*
Step 3: Develop Plan (including some contingency time) What tasks need to be done in order to complete writing? Who will do the writing?   *In house / outsourced (delete as appropriate)* Are any other writers involved?   *Yes / No (delete as appropriate)* *If Yes, who will write what and by when?* Critical Path Analysis *What tasks can be undertaken simultaneously?* *What tasks rely on (an)other task(s) to be completed first?* Set some interim deadline dates / time e.g. Writing time (Step 4); Checking time (Step 5); Publication time (Step 6)

Step 4: Create Content
If outsourced, has copy writer been fully briefed? *Yes / No / not applicable (delete as appropriate)*

Comments:

Step 5: Checking Process
Self-checking *(not recommended)*   *Yes / No (delete as appropriate)*
Independent in-house checker, e.g. work colleague   *Yes / No (delete as appropriate)*
Outsourced checker, e.g. proofreader   *Yes / No (delete as appropriate)*

Comments:

Step 6: Publication Process
In-house printing   *Yes / No (delete as appropriate)*
External printing   *Yes / No (delete as appropriate)*
No printing - electronic publication   *Yes / No (delete as appropriate)*

Deadline met?   *Yes / No / not applicable (delete as appropriate)*

Comments:

Step 7: Feedback monitoring and reporting
How will you gather feedback?

What actions will you take?

Comments:

This proforma has been designed to help you use the Business Writing Process Plan to plan your writing.

You can download the form from my website:

www.ppgproofreading.co.uk

I hope you find it useful.

Other Books by Peter Clarke

E-books

Historic Treasures of Uzbekistan - *Journey of Discovery Along the Silk Road*

Mughal India - *From the Taj to the Raj*

Visit Peter's website for links to online booksellers:
www.peterspocketguides.co.uk/publications

Peter's Pocket Guides

Coastal Norway

Discover China

Explore South Africa

Golden India

Uzbekistan

Visit Peter's website for more details:
www.peterspocketguides.co.uk

Stay Connected

You can connect with Peter in the following ways:

Follow him of Twitter:
@PPGProofreading
@PetersPktGuides

Like him on Facebook:
Facebook.com/PPGProofreading
Facebook.com/PetersPocketGuides

Connect on LinkedIn:
Linkedin.com/in/PeterClarke7

Visit his websites:
www.ppgproofreading.co.uk
www.peterspocketguides.co.uk